The Market Place, Cirencester by H. Sylvester Stannard R.A.

RECIPES

compiled by
Dorothy Baldock

SALMON

Index

Apricot Pudding 15
Bacon Pudding 46
Banbury Apple Pie 22
Banbury Cakes 37
Bibury Blackberry Pie 8
Boiled Cake 31
Cheltenham Pudding 19
Chestnut Chops 30
Cotswold Rabbit Pie 13
Crayfish and Bacon Savoury 14
Crundle Pudding 5
Duck in Port Wine 23
Egg and Bacon Pie 35
Friar's Omelette 6
Gloucester Cheese and Ale 29
Gloucester Pancakes 34
Gloucester Pot Spread 42
Gloucester Tartlets 47
Gloucestershire Pheasant Soup 21
Gloucestershire Ginger Cake 3
Gloucestershire Pie 24
Gloucestershire Squab Pie 45
Gooseberry Fool 38
Huntsman's Omelette 26
Mothering Sunday Pork 7
Oldbury Gooseberry Tarts 11
Painswick Gammon in Cider 32
Plum and Apple Dumpling 27
Plum Mould 18
Portmanteaued Chops 10
Spicy Mutton Pie 39
Stewed Kidneys 43
Sweet Gammon Pie 16
Tewkesbury Saucer Batters 40

Cover pictures: *front* Upper Slaughter
back Bourton-on-the-Hill by H. Sylvester Stannard R. A.
Printed and Published by J. Salmon Ltd., Sevenoaks, England ©

Gloucestershire Ginger Cake

3½ oz. butter or margarine
3 oz. soft brown sugar
4 oz. golden syrup
2 oz. black treacle
10 oz. flour
Pinch of salt
½ teaspoon bicarbonate of soda
2 teaspoons mixed spice
2 teaspoons ground ginger
1 egg, beaten
½ pint milk

Set oven to 375°F or Mark 5. Grease, flour and line a 1 lb. loaf tin. Melt the butter or the margarine, sugar, golden syrup and black treacle in a basin suspended over a saucepan of hot water. Mix together the flour, salt, bicarbonate of soda, mixed spice and ginger, and stir into the syrup mixture, combining well. Stir in the beaten egg and milk to form a soft, dropping consistency. Pour into the tin and bake for 1½ to 2 hours, or until well-risen and firm, covering the top with foil if it appears to be cooking too quickly.

The Stocks, Stow-on-the-Wold by H. Sylvester Stannard R.A.

Crundle Pudding

2 oz. flour
2 oz. butter, softened
2 oz. sugar
1 egg, beaten
½ pint warm milk
1 teaspoon ground nutmeg
Extra butter for 'dotting'

Set oven to 350°F or Mark 4. Rub the flour and butter together in a bowl until the mixture resembles fine breadcrumbs, then stir in the sugar. Beat the egg into the warm milk and stir into the flour mixture. Pour into a well buttered 2 pint pie dish, dot with a little extra butter, then sprinkle on the nutmeg. Bake for 30 to 40 minutes until golden brown. Serve accompanied by stewed apples or stewed plums. Serves 3 to 4.

Friar's Omelette

1 lb. cooking apples, peeled, cored and sliced
3 oz. butter
3 oz. granulated or soft brown sugar
Rind of half a lemon with 1 teaspoon lemon juice or ½ teaspoon ground nutmeg
2 eggs, beaten
4 oz. fresh white breadcrumbs

Set oven to 375°F or Mark 5. Butter a 1½ to 2 pint pie dish. Cook together the apples, butter, sugar and lemon rind and juice or the nutmeg, in a saucepan until soft, then beat to make a thick purée. Stir in the beaten eggs. Place half the breadcrumbs in the pie dish, spread the apple mixture over, then top with the remaining breadcrumbs. Dot with butter and sprinkle with a little extra sugar and cook for 30 to 40 minutes. Serve hot with custard or cold with whipped cream. Serves 4.

The name of this dish is nothing to do with the church, but is a corruption of 'fraise', the medieval version of an omelette. This is a very early version of Apple Charlotte.

Mothering Sunday Pork

A chine or loin of pork,
about 3 lb. in weight
Salt and lemon juice
Parsley sprigs
1 egg yolk
4 to 6 oz. fresh white breadcrumbs,
lightly seasoned with black pepper
1 oz. lard or dripping, melted
Parsley sprigs to garnish

Put the meat into cold water with a little salt and squeeze of lemon juice, bring to the boil and boil for 30 minutes. Drain and pat dry. Set oven to 425°F or Mark 7. With a sharp knife make a series of incisions in the meat, about 1 inch apart and stuff each with a parsley sprig, inserting the stalk first. Brush the meat all over with egg yolk, then coat with the seasoned breadcrumbs, patting them firmly into position. Set the meat on a rack in a roasting tin and baste with melted fat. Cook for 20 minutes to 'settle' the topping then reduce oven temperature to 350°F or Mark 4 and cook for a further 1 to 1½ hours. Serve garnished with parsley and with roast potatoes and broccoli or spinach, both traditional accompaniments. Serves 4 to 6.

Bibury Blackberry Pie

10 oz. shortcrust pastry
1 lb. blackberries, rinsed and drained very well
4 oz. soft brown sugar
½ level teaspoon ground cinnamon or nutmeg
A 'walnut' of butter
1 tablespoon sherry

Set oven to 400°F or Mark 6. Roll out the pastry on a lightly floured surface and use half to line a lightly buttered 10 inch pie plate. Layer the blackberries and the sugar blended with the spice, over the pastry base. Dot with the 'walnut' of butter and then sprinkle on the sherry. Cover with the remaining pastry, trimming the edges and sealing well. Decorate with the pastry trimmings and make a small 'steam hole' in the centre. Brush with a little milk or beaten egg to glaze and cook for about 30 to 35 minutes or until the pastry is golden. Serve hot with cream. Serves 4 to 6.

Arlington Row, Bibury by W. Carruthers Affleck

Portmanteaued Chops

4 loin of lamb chops, each about 1½ inches thick
8 chicken livers, trimmed and finely chopped
8 medium mushrooms, wiped and finely chopped
½ shallot, peeled and finely chopped
1 egg, beaten
2 oz. breadcrumbs
Salt and black pepper
1 oz. butter, melted

Set oven to 400°F or Mark 6. Using a sharp knife, slit the chops horizontally towards the bone to form a 'pocket'. Fry the chicken livers in a little melted butter, then add the mushrooms and shallot, and fry for about 5 minutes, stirring. Cool a little, then divide the mixture into 4 and use to stuff the chops. Sew up the chops, to keep the stuffing in place, then dip each into beaten egg. Mix the breadcrumbs and seasoning together and dip the chops into the mixture, pressing on the breadcrumbs firmly. Place the chops in an ovenproof dish and bake on one side for about 8 to 10 minutes, then turn over and bake for a further 10 minutes. Serve at once with grilled tomatoes or a fresh tomato sauce.

A popular hunting breakfast in days gone by.

Oldbury Gooseberry Tarts

1 lb. flour
PInch of salt
4oz. lard
4 oz. butter
5 tablespoons boiling water
About 12 to 14 oz. gooseberries, topped and tailed
6 oz. demerara sugar (or to taste)

Also known as Oldbury Gooseberry Pies, these tarts were traditionally sold at Whitsun Fairs in the Cotswolds, usually priced at 1 penny. They are best made the day before they are needed.

Sift the flour and salt together. Cut the lard and butter into small pieces and place in a bowl. Pour the boiling water over and stir briskly until the fats are dissolved. Shoot in the flour and beat hard to a stiffish, yet malleable dough. Turn on to a floured surface and roll out thinly. Using a saucer, cut out about 12 circles and smaller circles for lids. Pleat up the sides of the larger circles to form cases about 1 inch deep. Divide the gooseberries between the cases and sprinkle with sugar. Brush the edges of the cases and lids with water. Apply the lids, pinching edges well together. Make a 'steam hole' in each lid. Place on a lightly greased baking tray and leave in a cool place overnight to 'firm up' (this prevents collapsing during cooking). Set oven to 400°F or Mark 6. Brush with a little milk and bake for 15 to 20 minutes or until golden.

Bourton-on-the-Water by H. Sylvester Stannard R.A.

Cotswold Rabbit Pie

1 rabbit, jointed
Seasoned flour for dusting
1 oz. dripping
1 large onion, peeled and thickly sliced
2 carrots, peeled and sliced
1½ pints beef stock
Salt and black pepper
4 oz. mushrooms, wiped and thickly sliced (optional)
3 large slices of bread (with crusts on), quite thickly cut; about ½ inch or more
Chopped parsley to garnish

Set oven to 350°F or Mark 4. Dust the rabbit joints with seasoned flour. Melt the dripping and fry the joints on all sides to brown. Add the onion and carrots, then pour in the stock and bring to the boil. Season to taste. Transfer to an ovenproof casserole, cover and cook for about 1 to 1½ hours until the rabbit joints are tender. Add the mushrooms, if desired. Cut the bread slices in half diagonally, and dip into the gravy. Place on top of the casserole, gravy-side up, and cook for a further 40 minutes, uncovered, until the bread has become crisp. Serve, sprinkled with chopped parsley and accompanied by boiled potatoes. Serve 4.

A version of a very early 'poachers pie' with a bread rather than a pastry topping.

Crayfish and Bacon Savoury

8 oz. streaky bacon, de-rinded and chopped
8 oz. frozen crayfish tails, thawed
4 slices freshly-made toast
A little butter
Salt and black pepper
Chopped parsley to garnish

Fry the bacon gently, using as little fat as possible. Remove the meat from the crayfish tails, and chop finely. Add to the bacon, adding a little fat if necessary, and cook, stirring, for 5 minutes or until the crayfish is thoroughly heated through. Spread the toast with a little butter and place the slices on warmed plates. Season the crayfish and bacon mixture and divide between the slices of toast. Serve at once, garnished with chopped parsley, as a starter or a supper dish. Serves 4.

Apricot Pudding

1 large tin apricots in juice or
1½ lbs. fresh apricots, poached
2 oz. fresh white breadcrumbs
¼ pint single cream
1½ oz. sugar
2 eggs, beaten
1 tablespoon white wine, (optional)
1 teaspoon grated lemon rind
8 oz. shortcrust pastry

Although this recipe is termed an apricot 'pudding' it is really a form of apricot pie.

Set oven to 350°F or Mark 4. Drain the apricots well and sieve or process through a blender to purée. Place the breadcrumbs in a bowl, heat the cream thoroughly, but do not allow to boil, then stir into the breadcrumbs. Allow to cool, then stir in the sugar, beaten egg, wine if desired and lemon rind. Stir in the apricot purée and turn into a well-buttered, 1½ pint shallow pie dish or flan dish. Roll out the pastry on a lightly floured surface and use to cover the apricot filling, trimming it neatly and sealing the edges well. Use the trimmings to decorate and make a small 'steam hole' in the lid. Brush with a little milk or beaten egg to glaze and cook for 30 to 40 minutes until the pastry is golden. Sprinkle a little caster sugar on the lid. Serve hot, accompanied by custard or cream. Serves 4.

Sweet Gammon Pie

4 thick gammon rashers,
rinds removed and the fat nicked
to prevent curling
A 'walnut' of butter
6 oz. dried apricots, soaked overnight
then drained and cut in half
1 oz. sultanas
Black pepper
A little pork stock
1½ lb. potatoes
A little milk

Set oven to 375°F or Mark 5. Fry the gammon rashers in a little butter on both sides to seal and then place in a shallow ovenproof dish. Lay the apricot halves on top, then sprinkle the sultanas over and season with black pepper. Moisten with a little stock. Peel the potatoes, but leave whole. Put in a saucepan of salted water and bring to the boil. Boil for 5 minutes. Drain the potatoes very well, and cut into slices. Arrange the slices over the gammon, overlapping slightly, brush with milk and dot with butter. Cook for 50 minutes to 1 hour, covering the pie with foil if the potatoes appear to be browning too quickly. Serves 4.

Old Houses, Broadway by A. R. Quinton

Plum Mould

1 lb. plums
Finely grated rind of a lemon and 2 teaspoons lemon juice
2 tablespoons sugar
3 level teaspoons gelatine
¼ pint warm water
1 tablespoon port wine
½ pint double cream
2 egg whites
Whipped cream and flaked almonds to decorate

Wash the plums and cook in a very little water, to which the lemon rind and juice has been added, until soft. Remove the stones and sieve to purée the flesh. Dissolve the gelatine in the water then stir into the warm plum purée and allow to cool, but not set. Stir in the port wine. Whip the cream until it just holds its shape and fold into the plum purée. Whisk the egg whites until they stand in soft peaks and fold in. Put the mixture into a 2 to 2½ pint fancy mould or into a glass serving dish and refrigerate until set. Turn out of the mould and decorate either the mould or in the dish with rosettes of whipped cream 'spiked' with flaked almonds. Serve with boudoir or cat's tongue biscuits. Serves 4 to 6.

Cheltenham Pudding

6 oz. shredded suet
6 oz. flour
1 teaspoon baking powder
2 oz. fresh white breadcrumbs
4 oz. sultanas or raisins
2 oz. currants
½ teaspoon ground nutmeg
Grated rind of ½ lemon
2 eggs, beaten
Milk

Set oven to 375°F or Mark 5. Mix together the suet, flour, baking powder, breadcrumbs, fruit, nutmeg and lemon rind in a bowl. Make a well in the mixture and add the beaten eggs. Combine well together, then add sufficient milk to form a stiff, yet smooth batter. Turn into a well buttered 2½ to 3 pint pie dish, and bake for 1 to 1½ hours until golden. Serve with jam or lemon sauce. Serves 4 to 6.

Old Almshouses, Chipping Campden by W. Carruthers Affleck

Gloucestershire Clear Pheasant Soup

1 pheasant, cleaned and jointed
1 large onion, peeled and roughly chopped
2 carrots, peeled and sliced
1 leek, washed, trimmed and sliced
2 sticks celery, wiped, trimmed and chopped
6 sprigs parsley, 2 sprigs thyme and a bayleaf, tied together with string
1 blade of mace
12 peppercorns
Salt
2 teaspoons lemon juice
4 tablespoons port or sherry
1 stick celery, wiped trimmed and finely diced

Place the pheasant joints, onion, carrots, leek, celery, herbs, mace and peppercorns in a large saucepan. Add salt to taste and one teaspoonful of the lemon juice. Add sufficient cold water to cover. Cover and bring to the boil, then simmer over a *very* gentle heat for 4 hours. Strain well, reserving the best pieces of pheasant meat. Allow to get cold, then skim off all the surface fat. Dice the reserved meat. Pour the soup into a saucepan, add the diced pheasant meat and bring to the boil. Stir in the port or sherry. Serve the soup garnished with the finely diced celery, that has been blanched in boiling water to which 1 teaspoon of lemon juice has been added. Serve with fingers of hot toast. Serves 4.

Banbury Apple Pie

12 oz. shortcrust pastry
1½ lb. cooking apples, peeled, cored and sliced
Juice of ½ lemon
4 oz. sultanas
½ oz. candied peel (optional)
3 oz. soft brown sugar
Pinch ground cinnamon
Pinch ground nutmeg
Rind and juice of ½ an orange

Set oven to 400°F or Mark 6. Roll out the pastry on a lightly floured surface and use to line a buttered, shallow 1½ pint pie dish, reserving the remainder for the lid. Sprinkle the apples with lemon juice and fill the pie with layers of apple, sultanas, peel, sugar and spices. Sprinkle the orange rind and juice over and cover with the remaining pastry, trimming the edges neatly and pressing together firmly. Make a small 'steam hole' in the centre of the lid and decorate with the pastry trimmings. Brush with a little milk or beaten egg to glaze and cook for 30 minutes or until golden brown. Sprinkle the top with a little sifted icing sugar. Serve hot or cold, accompanied by custard or cream. Serves 4 to 6.

Duck in Port Wine

1 oven-prepared duck, about 4 lb.
8 small apples, peeled and cored
½ bottle of port wine
Juice of a small lemon
1 oz. butter
1 tablespoon flour
PInch of dry mustard powder
Salt and black pepper
1 teaspoon finely grated lemon rind
½ pint chicken stock

The day before, prepare apples and place in basin with port and lemon juice. Cover and leave in cool place. Next day, set oven to 400°F or Mark 7. Wipe duck inside and out and season cavity. Rub skin with a little butter. Mix flour, mustard, seasoning and lemon rind and rub into skin. Put remaining butter in roasting tin with the duck. Roast 40 minutes, basting occasionally. Drain port from apples into a pan and heat through: do not boil. Baste duck with 2 or 3 tablespoons of port every 5 minutes until all used (30 to 40 minutes). Place apples around duck and cook further 20 minutes. Meanwhile, heat stock and baste duck and apples 2 or 3 times. Remove apples; keep warm. Drain liquid into a pan and return duck to oven for further 10 to 15 minutes. Mix roasting liquid with remaining stock and heat. Place duck on dish, with apples. Pour on port and serve remainder separately. Serves 4.

Gloucestershire Pie

1 lb. lean lamb, cooked and sliced
1 lb. onions, peeled and thinly sliced
1 lb. cooking apples, peeled, cored and thinly sliced
2 oz. butter
Pinch of rosemary and nutmeg
½ pint rich brown gravy
½–¾ lb. potatoes, peeled and diced
½–¾ lb. swede, peeled and diced
Salt and pepper

Set oven to 375°F or Mark 5. Put the onions and apples in a pan and cover with water. Boil for 5 minutes. Drain well. Meanwhile boil the swede for 10 minutes, then add the potatoes, and cook until both are soft. Drain well and mash them together until smooth. Grease an ovenproof dish with the butter. Place layers of the meat and the onion and apple mixture alternately in the dish, seasoning and sprinkling each layer with herbs as it fills up. Pour in the gravy and top with the mashed potato and swede mixture. Dot the top with butter and bake, uncovered, for ¾ – 1 hour. Serve with a green vegetable. Serves 4.

Fairford Mill by H. Sylvester Stannard R.A.

Huntsman's Omelette

4 oz. fresh white breadcrumbs
Salt and black pepper
A little grated nutmeg
3 fl oz. double cream
4 oz. butter
1 onion, peeled and chopped
2 oz. mushrooms, wiped and sliced
2 oz. lamb's liver, trimmed and finely chopped
2 lamb's kidneys, skinned, cored and finely chopped
8 eggs, beaten
Parsley sprigs to garnish

A Gloucestershire recipe that is strictly an egg dish, rather than a 'classic' omelette.

Mix together the breadcrumbs, seasoning, nutmeg and cream and leave to stand for 30 minutes. Melt half the butter and fry the onion and mushrooms until soft. Remove and keep warm. Add the liver and kidney to the butter and fry, stirring, for 4 to 5 minutes. Mix with the onion and mushrooms and keep warm. Beat the eggs into the breadcrumb mixture. In a large frying pan melt the remaining butter and, as soon as it begins to foam, pour in the egg mixture. Cook in the same way as an omelette, drawing the sides into the middle, for 2 minutes. Spoon the liver mixture into the centre, dot with a little butter, if desired, and place under a preheated grill for 1 minute until the egg mixture 'fluffs' up. Divide into four pieces, garnish each with parsley and serve immediately. Serves 4.

Plum and Apple 'Dumpling'

8 oz. flour
1 teaspoon baking powder
Pinch of salt
4 oz. shredded suet
¼ pint water
1 lb. plums, washed and stoned
8 oz. cooking apples, peeled, cored and sliced
6 oz. sugar
1 tablespoon stale sponge cake crumbs or fresh white breadcrumbs
1 tablespoon water to which a teaspoon lemon juice has been added
A 'walnut' of butter

Traditionally served on St. Margaret's Day, 20th July, this pudding is known in Gloucestershire as Heg-Peg-Dump!

Mix the flour, baking powder and salt into a bowl, then stir in the suet. Add the water and mix to a soft dough. Turn out on to a lightly floured surface, knead lightly, then roll out and use to line a buttered 2 pint pudding basin, reserving a portion of the dough for a lid. Fill the basin with alternating layers of plums, apples and sugar, sprinkling the crumbs in between. Add the water and the 'walnut' of butter. Top with the reserved dough, damping the edges and pressing down well to seal. Cover with buttered greaseproof paper and tie down. Steam for 2½ to 3 hours, topping up the water as necessary. Serve with custard or cream. Serves 4 to 6.

The New Inn, Gloucester by A. R. Quinton

Gloucester Cheese and Ale

6 oz. double Gloucester cheese, thinly sliced
1 teaspoon made English mustard
About 4 to 4½ fl oz. brown ale
4 thick slices of bread, freshly toasted

Set oven to 375°F or Mark 5. Arrange the cheese slices in the bottom of a lightly buttered ovenproof dish and spread on the mustard. Pour on sufficient ale just to cover the cheese. Cover with foil and cook for about 10 minutes or until the cheese has softened and mingled with the ale. Pour the cheese and ale mixture over the toasted bread and serve at once. Serves 4.

A popular savoury served to travellers at coaching inns or posting houses.

Chestnut Chops

16 to 20 chestnuts
4 large lamb chops
1 oz. dripping
2 onions, peeled and finely sliced
2 tablespoons flour
¾ pint lamb stock
1 wineglass white wine, (optional)
½ teaspoon dried thyme
Salt and black pepper

If preferred, pork chops can be used instead of lamb chops.

Set oven to 350°F or Mark 4. Split the skins of the chestnuts and cook them in hot water for about 5 minutes, then, whilst still warm, remove the outer skins and thin membranes. Trim the lamb chops, and dust with seasoned flour. Melt the dripping and fry the chops lightly on both sides to seal. Place in an ovenproof casserole. Add the onions to the remaining dripping and fry until soft. Stir in the flour and cook for 1 to 2 minutes, then add the stock, with the wine if desired, the thyme and seasoning and, stirring, bring to the boil. Add the chestnuts to the chops in the casserole, then pour in the stock. Cover and cook for 50 minutes to 1 hour. Serve with boiled potatoes and a green vegetable, traditionally cabbage. Serves 4.

Boiled Cake

3 oz. butter
2 oz. granulated sugar
1 oz. golden syrup
½ pint water
3 to 4 oz. sultanas
10 oz. flour
3 teaspoons baking powder
Pinch of salt
1 teaspoon mixed spice
1 teaspoon bicarbonate of soda

Set oven to 350°F or Mark 4. Grease line the base of an 8 inch cake tin. Put the sugar, syrup, water and sultanas into a saucepan and heat until the butter has melted; then boil for 2 minutes and allow to cool until lukewarm. Mix together the flour, baking powder, salt, spice and bicarbonate of soda, pour into the fruit mixture and beat well together. Turn into the cake tin, smooth over the top and bake for 1¼ to 1½ hours, or until a skewer inserted into the cake comes out clean. Cover the top with foil if the cake appears to be browning too quickly. Allow to cool in the tin for 5 minutes, then turn out on to a wire rack.

...nswick Gammon in Cider

4 gammon rashers, rinds removed and the fat nicked to prevent curling
1 level tablespoon made English mustard
1 oz. demerara sugar
½ pint dry, still cider
½ oz. butter
1½ oz. tablespoons flour
Salt and black pepper (optional)
Parsley sprigs to garnish

Set oven to 400°F or Mark 6. Mix together the mustard and sugar with enough cider to make a smooth paste. Spread over the rashers and leave for 30 minutes. Place the rashers in a large ovenproof dish and cook for 15 minutes. Melt the butter in a saucepan and stir in the flour together with the seasoning if desired. Add the remaining cider and cook, stirring continuously, until the sauce has boiled and is smooth and thick. Pour over the rashers, and cook for a further 15 minutes. Serve garnished with parsley sprigs. Serves 4.

If preferred, bacon chops can be used in place of the gammon rashers.

An old corner, Painswick by H. Sylvester Stannard R.A.

Gloucester Pancakes

6 oz. flour
Pinch of salt
1 level teaspoon baking powder
3 oz. shredded suet
1 egg, beaten
A little milk
Lard for frying

Stir together the flour, salt and baking powder in a bowl then rub in the suet. Add the egg and sufficient milk to produce a stiff dough. Roll out on a lightly floured surface to about ½ inch thick, then cut into about 12 rounds, using a plain, (not fluted) 2 inch cutter. Melt a little lard in a frying pan and fry the cakes until golden brown on both sides. Drain well and serve at once with warmed golden syrup or a lemon sauce. Makes about 12 cakes.

This Cotswold pudding is not prepared with a batter, but with a suet dough and it is the suet that gives them their attractive 'sandy' texture.

Egg and Bacon Pie

12 oz. puff pastry
1 lb. lean bacon rashers, de-rinded and diced
6 eggs
Salt and black pepper

Set oven to 425°F or Mark 7. Roll out the pastry on a lightly floured surface and use half to line a buttered 7 inch pie plate. Sprinkle half the diced bacon over the pastry base. Break the eggs over the bacon (if preferred the eggs may be beaten before being poured over the bacon). Sprinkle on the remaining bacon and season to taste. Cover the pie with the remainder of the pastry, trimming and sealing the edges well. Brush with a little milk or beaten egg to glaze. Bake for 10 minutes, then reduce the oven temperature to 350°F or Mark 4 for a further 20 to 25 minutes or until the pastry is well-risen and golden. Serve the pie hot with potatoes and peas or cold with salad. Serves 4 to 6.

The Old Cake Shop, Banbury by W. Carruthers Affleck

Banbury Cakes

1 lb. puff pastry
2 oz. butter, melted
4 oz. raisins
4 oz. currants
2 oz. mixed peel
4 oz. demerara sugar
1 level teaspoon mixed spice
Egg white and caster sugar for topping

Set oven to 425°F or Mark 7. Mix the melted butter, fruit, peel, sugar and spice together in a bowl, combining well. Roll out the pastry on a lightly floured surface and, using a saucer, cut into about 16 circles. Divide the fruit mixture evenly between them, then dampen the edges of the pastry circles and draw up into the centre, sealing well. Turn over and, with the hands, gently form the cakes into ovals, then press down very gently with a rolling pin. Make 3 diagonal cuts across the top of each cake, then brush with egg white and sprinkle with sugar. Place on lightly greased baking trays and bake for 15 to 20 minutes or until golden. Serve slightly warm. Makes about 16.

These oval cakes date back to Tudor days, and were originally sold from special lidded baskets and wrapped in white cloths to keep them warm.

Gooseberry Fool

2 lb. gooseberries, topped and tailed
4 to 6 oz. sugar, (or to taste)
1 head of elderflowers, well rinsed and the stem removed
½ pint double cream
½ pint made cold custard
Chopped almonds and extra double cream for decoration

Gooseberry Fool was a popular dessert as early as the 15th century, and gooseberries were traditionally eaten at Whitsuntide. A head of elderflower stewed with the gooseberries gives them a delicate Muscat flavour and is a popular country tradition.

Simmer the gooseberries in a little water until soft, then stir in the sugar and add the elderflower head. Cook gently until all the sugar is dissolved. Remove the elderflower head and sieve the gooseberries to make a smooth purée. Allow to cool. Whip the cream very lightly. Fold the cold custard into the gooseberry purée, then fold in the cream. Spoon into a glass bowl or 4 to 6 individual glass dishes and serve, chilled, decorated with rosettes of whipped cream and chopped nuts and accompanied by boudoir or cat's tongue biscuits. Serves 4 to 6.

Spicy Mutton Pie

12 oz. shortcrust pastry
Seasoned flour for dusting
8 oz. boned mutton or lamb
1 oz. dripping
8 oz. cooking apples, peeled, cored and chopped (weighed after preparation)
A little lemon juice
1½ oz. soft brown sugar or granulated sugar
1½ to 2 oz. currants
1 teaspoon ground nutmeg
A 'walnut' of butter
Salt and black pepper

The sheep of the Cotswolds, because of their long curly fleeces, were sometimes nicknamed 'Cotswold Lions'. The filling of this pie is a mixture of savoury and sweet.

Set oven to 375°F or Mark 5. Cut the meat into small cubes and dust with seasoned flour. Melt the dripping and brown the meat to seal. Remove and drain well. Rinse the chopped apple in a little water, to which a little lemon juice has been added, and drain well. Place a layer of meat in the bottom of a 1½ to 2 pint pie dish and top with a layer of apple. Sprinkle half the sugar and currants over with a little nutmeg, then repeat the layers. Dot with butter and season with salt and black pepper. Roll out the pastry on a lightly floured surface and use to cover the pie, trimming and sealing well. Make a small 'steam hole' in the lid and brush with a little milk or beaten egg to glaze. Cook for 40 to 50 minutes or until the pastry is golden brown. Serve with a selection of vegetables and a thin gravy. Serves 4.

Tewkesbury Saucer Batters

2 eggs
3 oz. flour
Pinch of salt
1 oz. sugar
½ pint milk
Stewed soft fruit,
apples, plums, raspberries etc.

Set oven to 400°F or Mark 6. Separate the eggs. Mix together the flour, salt and sugar. Make a well in the centre and add the egg yolks and the milk. Beat to a smooth batter. Whisk the egg whites until they will just hold their shape and fold in. Butter 8 to 10 large ovenproof saucers and divide the batter between them. Bake for 15 to 20 minutes. Place half the batters on warmed serving plates, and top with soft fruit. Place the remaining batters on top of each and serve at once, sprinkled, if desired, with a little sifted icing sugar, Serves 4 to 5.

If preferred, large batters can be made by using ovenproof plates, and the batters then served cut into portions.

Tewkesbury Abbey from the Meadows by A. R. Quinton

Gloucester Pot Spread

2 lb. blade bone steak
4 tablespoons red wine
1 level teaspoon mustard powder
1 level teaspoon strong horseradish sauce
3 level teaspoons finely chopped parsley
Salt and black pepper

Trim the meat, removing any fat, then slice *very* thinly, using a sharp knife. Place in a dish. Combine together the wine, mustard powder, horseradish and parsley and season lightly. Pour over the sliced meat, cover and leave in a cool place overnight. Pack the meat in a large stone jar or a heatproof container, and pour in any remaining juices. Cover the top with foil and press down, but do not tie down. Stand the jar or container on a trivet in a saucepan of simmering water and cook for about 8 hours, topping up the water as necessary. Allow to get cold, when the meat will have set. Serve as a spread, spooned from its container, with crusty bread or hot toast. Serves 4 to 8.

This tasty meat paste is sometimes called Gloucestershire 'Stew'.

Stewed Kidneys

12 lamb's kidneys, skinned, cored, and halved
Seasoned flour
1½ oz. butter
1½ pints rich brown stock
3 sprigs parsley, 1 sprig of thyme and a bayleaf, tied together with string
2 onions, peeled and cut into rings
2 tart cooking apples, peeled, cored and cut into thick rings
1½ oz. butter
1 level tablespoon cornflour
Salt and black pepper
Chopped parsley to garnish

Set oven to 300°F or Mark 2. Dip the kidneys in well-seasoned flour. Melt the butter and fry the kidneys quickly on both sides to seal. Place in an ovenproof casserole. Bring the stock to the boil and pour over the kidneys. Add the herbs, cover and place in the oven. Fry the onion and apple rings in the butter for 2 to 3 minutes, and add to the casserole. Lower the oven temperature to 250°F or Mark ½ and cook for 4 hours. Before serving, thicken the gravy with the cornflour, which has been mixed to a smooth paste with a little water, remove the herbs and season lightly. Serve garnished with chopped parsley and accompanied by thick slices of hot, fresh toast. Serves 4.

The River Windrush, Burford by H. Sylvester Stannard R.A.

Gloucestershire Squab Pie

8 oz. shortcrust pastry
12 small best-end-of-neck lamb cutlets
1 large cooking apple, peeled, cored and sliced
2 onions, peeled and sliced
Salt and black pepper
½ teaspoon ground nutmeg
¼ pint lamb stock

Set oven to 400°F or Mark 6. Place half the lamb in a 1½ to 2 pint pie dish and layer half the apple and onion slices on top. Sprinkle with seasoning and nutmeg, then place the remainder of the lamb and the apple and onion slices on top. Pour on the stock. Roll out the pastry on a lightly floured surface and cover the pie, trimming the edges neatly and sealing well. Use trimmings for decoration and make a small 'steam hole' in the centre of the lid. Brush with milk or beaten egg to glaze. Bake for 20 minutes, then lower the oven temperature to 350°F or Mark 4 and cook for a further 1 to 1¼ hours. Serve with creamed potatoes and carrots. Serves 4.

Bacon Pudding

1 lb. suet pastry
1 lb. streaky bacon rashers, de-rinded
2 onions, peeled and chopped
½ teaspoon fresh sage, chopped
2 teaspoons fresh parsley, chopped
Black pepper

Roll out the suet pastry on a lightly floured surface to form a square 6–8 inches in size and about ¼–½ inch thick. Lay the bacon rashers over the pastry, overlapping each one slightly, then spread on the chopped onion. Mix the sage and parsley together, sprinkle over and season with black pepper. Roll up the pastry, Swiss Roll fashion, and seal well. Wrap in lightly buttered greaseproof paper and steam for about 3 hours, topping up the water as necessary. Serve cut into thick slices, with a brown gravy and accompanied by boiled potatoes and turnips, the traditional vegetables for this dish. Serves 4 to 6.

Gloucester Tartlets

6 oz. shortcrust pastry
2 oz. butter, softened
2 oz. sugar
A few drops of almond essence
1 egg, beaten
2 oz. ground rice
Raspberry or apricot jam

Set oven to 375°F or Mark 5. Roll out the pastry on a lightly floured surface and use to line about 16 lightly greased and floured patty tins. Cream the butter and sugar together, then stir in the almond essence and the egg. Fold in the ground rice and combine well. Place a little jam in each pastry case and top with a good spoonful of the ground rice mixture. Cook for 15 to 20 minutes or until the filling is golden and springy to the touch. Cool on a wire rack and, before serving, dust with a little sifted icing sugar. Makes about 16 tarts.

A Cotswold version of Swiss Tarts

METRIC CONVERSIONS

The weights, measures and oven temperatures used in the preceding recipes can be easily converted to their metric equivalents. The conversions listed below are only approximate, having been rounded up or down as may be appropriate.

Weights

Avoirdupois	Metric
1 oz.	just under 30 grams
4 oz. (¼ lb.)	app. 115 grams
8 oz. (½ lb.)	app. 230 grams
1 lb.	454 grams

Liquid Measures

Imperial	Metric
1 tablespoon (liquid only)	20 millilitres
1 fl. oz.	app. 30 millilitres
1 gill (¼ pt.)	app. 145 millilitres
½ pt.	app. 285 millilitres
1 pt.	app. 570 millilitres
1 qt.	app. 1.140 litres

Oven Temperatures

	°Fahrenheit	Gas Mark	°Celsius
Slow	300	2	150
	325	3	170
Moderate	350	4	180
	375	5	190
	400	6	200
Hot	425	7	220
	450	8	230
	475	9	240

Flour as specified in these recipes refers to Plain Flour unless otherwise described.